CLASSIC
Main Dishes
HOME COOKING

S0-CAO-211

Publications International, Ltd.
Favorite Brand Name Recipes at www.fbnr.com

Pictured on the front cover: Veal Piccata with Fennel *(page 36).*

ISBN: 0-7853-7804-9

Manufactured in China.

8 7 6 5 4 3 2 1

Microwave Cooking: Microwave ovens vary in wattage. Use the cooking times as guidelines and check for doneness before adding more time.

CONTENTS

Hungarian Beef Goulash (*page 24*)

Jamaican Baby Back Ribs (*page 46*)

Lemon-Garlic Shish Kabobs (*page 58*)

CLASS NOTES

It's time to get back to the basics of meat and potatoes! Meat is leaner than ever, according to the National Live Stock & Meat Board. Beef is 27% leaner than it was just 20 years ago thanks to leaner animals and closer trimming of fat. Pork is 50% leaner than it was in the late 1960's due to better feeding practices and improved genetics, according to the U.S. Department of Agriculture (USDA). And because of the wide variety of meat cuts available, meat now can be prepared even more quickly.

So what better way to warm up on a cold night than with the hearty recipes found here? *Classic Home Cooking Main Dishes* shows you dozens of ways to prepare beef, veal, pork and lamb with step-by-step directions and clear how-to photos. Take a few minutes to read the information below to help you choose and prepare the best possible meat for your next meal.

SELECTING MEAT

All meat sold in supermarkets and retail shops must be federally or state inspected for wholesomeness. In order to ensure you are buying the freshest meat possible, look for packages that are securely wrapped with no signs of leakage, excess liquid or tears. The meat also should be cold to the touch. Always check the "sell-by" date and purchase only on or before that date. In addition, look for cuts that are uniform in size so that they cook evenly.

Beef: Beef is graded by the USDA. *Prime* is well-marbled meat, usually destined for restaurants and specialty markets. *Choice* is the everyday grade, forming over 60% of production. *Select* has less fat and provides fewer calories but may not be as tender as prime or choice. When choosing beef, look for: 1) marbling or flecks and thin streaks of fat that run throughout a piece of beef, enhancing its tenderness, juiciness and flavor, 2) a bright, cherry-red color (avoid meat with a grayish tone or yellow fat), 3) beef that is firm to the touch and 4) the cut. Cuts marked "loin" or "rib" tend to be more tender, while chuck, round and flank tend to be less tender.

Veal: Veal is meat from calves that weigh 350 pounds or less and are not older than three months. These calves usually have a diet that consists only of milk. When choosing veal, look for: 1) light pink color with fine-grained, velvety texture and little fat (avoid meat with dry or brown spots or a reddish or gray color) and 2) fat that is milky white.

Pork: When choosing pork, look for: 1) moist meat that is pink in color (avoid meat with dry or discolored surfaces or a reddish or gray color), 2) fat that is milky white and 3) the cut. Cuts marked "loin" or "leg" tend to be leaner. Lean cuts include tenderloin, loin chop and sirloin roast. (Check labels for cured or smoked pork cuts such as hams or sausages to see if the meat is "fully-cooked" or if it needs to be "cooked-before-eating.")

Lamb: At one time, the delicate flavor of lamb was only available in the spring. Today lamb is available year round. Lamb is marketed when it is six to eight months old. When choosing lamb, look for: 1) bones that are small and 2) moist meat that is light pink in color (avoid meat that is red).

COOKING METHODS

Roasting: Place the meat, fat side up, on a rack in an open roaster. Do not add water. Insert a meat thermometer (technique on page 20) and roast in the oven at 300° to 350°F until the meat thermometer registers 10°F *below* the desired doneness. Allow the meat to stand for 15 minutes before carving. This method is best for large cuts of meat, at least 2 inches thick, such as roasts and hams. The following timetable will help you determine approximate roasting times.

Cut of Meat	Weight (pounds)	Oven Temperature	Cooking Time (minutes/pound)
Beef Rib Roast	4 to 6	325°F	26 to 30 (rare)
			34 to 38 (medium)
	6 to 8	325°F	23 to 25 (rare)
			27 to 30 (medium)
	8 to 10	325°F	19 to 21 (rare)
			23 to 25 (medium)
Beef Tenderloin, whole	4 to 6	425°F	45 to 60 minutes total
Beef Top Round Roast	2½ to 4	325°F	25 to 30 (rare)
			30 to 35 (medium)
	4 to 6	325°F	20 to 25 (rare)
			25 to 30 (medium)
Veal Loin Roast, boneless	2 to 3	300° to 325°F	18 to 20 (medium)
			22 to 24 (well)
Veal Rump Roast, boneless	2 to 3	300° to 325°F	33 to 35 (medium)
			37 to 40 (well)
Veal Shoulder Roast, boneless	2½ to 3	300° to 325°F	31 to 34 (medium)
			34 to 37 (well)
Lamb Leg, bone-in	7 to 9	325°F	15 to 20 (rare)
			20 to 25 (medium)
			25 to 30 (well)
Lamb Rib Roast	2 to 3	375°F	25 to 30 (rare)
			30 to 35 (medium)
			35 to 40 (well)
Pork Tenderloin	½ to 1	425°F	27 to 29
Pork Loin Top Loin Roast (double, boneless)	3 to 4	325°F	29 to 34
Pork Loin Top Loin Roast (boneless)	2 to 4	325°F	23 to 33
Pork Crown Roast	6 to 10	325°F	20 to 25
Pork Leg or Fresh Ham (whole, bone-in)	12	325°F	23 to 25
Fully-Cooked Boneless Ham (with ½ cup water; covered)	1½ to 2	325°F	29 to 33
	3 to 4	325°F	19 to 23
	6 to 8	325°F	16 to 20
	9 to 11	325°F	12 to 16

Broiling/Grilling: Preheat the broiler or prepare the grill (technique on page 43). Place the meat on the rack in the broiler pan so that fat can drip off during cooking or directly on the grid of the grill. Place thin cuts (³/₄ to 1 inch thick) two to three inches and thicker cuts three to six inches from the heat source. If broiling or grilling less tender cuts, such as flank, marinate the meat first. This method is best for steaks, chops, ground meat, ribs and cubed meat for kabobs. Smaller roasts, such as pork and beef tenderloin, also work well with this method, but prepare the grill for indirect cooking.

Panbroiling: Sometimes referred to as "frying without fat," this method is a quick way to prepare ground patties, cutlets and steaks less than 1 inch thick on the range top. Cook, uncovered, in a preheated nonstick skillet.

Panfrying: Sometimes referred to as "sautéing," this method is similar to panbroiling except a small amount of oil is added to the pan. Use this method for tender cuts, steaks and ground patties. Cook, uncovered, over medium heat until done, turning occasionally.

Stir-Frying: This is a variation of panfrying. This method is a fast way to cook meat that is cut in uniform small pieces with other foods, such as vegetables. Stir-frying is best done in a large skillet or wok over medium-high heat, adding just enough oil to coat the skillet. Cook the meat in batches, if necessary, to avoid overcrowding. Meat and other ingredients must be kept in constant motion by stirring or tossing vigorously. Once cooking is completed, remove from heat immediately.

Braising: With this method, first brown the meat in a heavy skillet or Dutch oven, then add a small amount of liquid. Bring the liquid to a simmer and cook, tightly covered, until the meat is tender. It is important not to let the liquid boil and to cook the meat at a low, even temperature to prevent the meat from becoming tough. The liquid can be thickened with flour to make gravy, if desired. Roasts, ribs, tougher cuts of steaks, shanks and briskets are all good cuts for braising.

Cooking in Liquid: This is similar to braising but after browning, the meat is completely covered with a liquid, such as water or broth. Other ingredients, such as vegetables and pasta, can be added. Bring the liquid to a simmer and cook, tightly covered, until the meat is tender. This method is used for making soups and stews but also can be used to poach or simmer other cuts of meat. Cuts of meat that work best include shanks, shank cross cuts, stew meat, ribs, pork hocks and tough roasts.

HOW MUCH TO BUY

The amount of meat to purchase per serving varies according to the cut. The following chart is a general guideline for determining servings per pound for beef, veal, pork and lamb.

Cut	Servings per Pound (3 ounces cooked, trimmed)
Boneless (such as sirloin, fillet, ground, stew, boneless cutlet and roast)	3 to 4
Bone-in (such as T-bone steak, rib/loin chops, shoulder roast)	2 to 3
Very Bony (such as ribs, shanks, riblets)	1 to 1¹/₂

STORING AND FREEZING

Cuts of beef, veal, pork and lamb can be refrigerated (36° to 40°F) in their original packaging for three to four days. However ground meat should only be held in the refrigerator for up to two days. Deli meats, such as sliced ham, corned beef, roast beef, bacon, frankfurters and fully-cooked sausages, can be refrigerated in their original vacuum-sealed packages for up to two weeks (always check expiration dates). If these meats are deli wrapped, store for only three to five days. Store fresh, uncooked sausage in the refrigerator for two to three days, even if vacuum sealed.

If you cannot use the meat within the recommended time, freeze it *immediately* after purchasing by wrapping it tightly with coated freezer paper. Airtight packaging is the key to successful freezing. Freeze meat at 0°F or colder for 6 to 12 months, depending on the size of the cut. Larger cuts of meat, such as roasts, have less area exposed to the air and therefore can be frozen longer. Smaller cuts of meat, such as cutlets, risk freezer burn more quickly since they have more surface area exposed to the air. Ground meat can be frozen for up to three months. Deli meats, fresh pork sausage links and patties, luncheon meats and frankfurters can be wrapped in freezer paper and frozen for up to two months. Use bacon within one month of freezing. Leftover cooked meat can be safely refrigerated for three days or frozen for up to three months in an airtight container.

SAFE FOOD HANDLING HINTS

Follow this list of precautions when handling meat to avoid food-related illnesses.

• To thaw meat, place the meat in the refrigerator overnight. Do *not* defrost meat at room temperature as this promotes bacteria growth.

• Remove the meat from the refrigerator just before cooking; it is not necessary to bring meat to room temperature first.

• Cutting boards and knives used for preparing raw meat must be scrubbed thoroughly with hot soapy water before and after using. Bacteria from the meat can be transferred to work areas, utensils or hands and could contaminate other foods that touch the same surfaces.

• Cook meat to the USDA recommended temperature (see page 10).

• Promptly store leftovers (see above); do not cool leftovers on counter first.

IS IT DONE YET?

The best way to determine if meat is cooked properly is to use a thermometer. There are two types of thermometers that can be used for meat: 1) a meat thermometer, which is inserted into the meat before cooking and is left in during cooking, and 2) an instant-read thermometer, which is inserted into the meat for about 10 seconds and then removed. Instant-read thermometers are *not* heatproof, so do not leave them in the meat while cooking. Test with an instant-read thermometer at the recommended minimum cooking time.

When using a thermometer, insert it into the thickest part of the meat, not touching bone or fat. For larger cuts of meat, such as roasts, it is recommended that the meat be cooked until the thermometer registers 5° to 10°F *below* desired doneness. Allow roasts to stand about 15 minutes before carving. During the standing time, roasts will continue to rise 5° to 10°F. Begin carving when the thermometer registers the desired temperature (see page 10).

The following chart shows the USDA recommended temperatures for meat doneness.

Type of Meat	Recommended Temperature
Beef (all cuts but ground)	
Rare	140°F
Medium-Rare	150°F
Medium	160°F
Well-Done	170°F
Very Well-Done	180°F
Ground Beef	160°–170°F
Pork/Veal	
Medium	160°F
Well-Done	170°F
Ham	
Fully-Cooked Ham	140°F
Uncooked Ham	170°F
Lamb	
Rare	140°F
Medium	160°F
Well-Done	170°F

The USDA recommends cooking ground beef to at least medium doneness (160°F) or until centers of hamburgers are no longer pink and the juices run clear. Other cuts of beef can be cooked to desired doneness because the bacteria tend to be on the outside of the meat. With most cuts, the bacteria get "seared" off during cooking. With ground meat, however, the bacteria also may be in the center of the meat. For steaks and thin cuts of meat, it may be easier to check for doneness by cutting a small slit in the meat and looking at the color of the meat near the bone or in the center of a boneless cut. If checking beef or lamb, use the following visual guide. (Veal cutlets should be cooked until tender and barely pink in the center.)

Rare—Bright red in center, pink toward outer edges
Medium—Light pink in center, brown on outer edges
Well-Done—Uniform brown throughout

Pork does not need to be cooked to 180°F as once thought. To keep pork juicy, cook it to medium (it will be faintly pink in center, but safe to eat) or to well-done (it will lose almost all of its pink color, but still be juicy).

CARVING

Once you have prepared the meat, you will want to carve the main attraction like a pro. Follow these helpful guidelines and illustrations.

General Guidelines

• Allow enough time before serving not only for cooking the meat, but for stand time and carving.

• Allow large cuts of meat to stand about 15 minutes. Stand time allows the meat to finish cooking, and the meat is easier to carve after standing. If the meat is carved immediately out of the oven, it loses more of its flavorful juices.

• Unless you are planning on carving at the table, place the meat on a large cutting board with a well at one end to hold the juice. (Or place a cutting board inside a baking sheet with a rim. The juice will collect in the baking sheet.) Use a long, sharp carving knife to slice the meat and a long-handled meat fork to steady the meat.

Boneless Roasts

Boneless beef, veal, pork and lamb roasts are easy to carve. Hold the roast steady with a long-handled meat fork. With the knife held perpendicular to the cutting board, cut across the grain into thin uniform slices. Cut the slices between $1/4$ to $1/2$ inch thick.

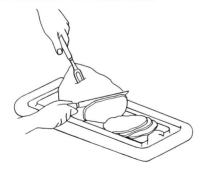

Beef brisket and flank steak are thinner cuts of meat. Follow the preceding directions, but slice the meat diagonally across the grain.

Standing Beef Rib Roast

For added stability, cut a wedge-shaped slice from the large end of the roast so that the meat will sit flat on the cutting board. Insert a long-handled meat fork below the top rib. Slice across the top of the roast toward the rib bone. This roast can be sliced between $1/2$ to $3/4$ inch thick.

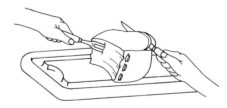

With the tip of the knife, cut along the rib bone to release the slice of meat.

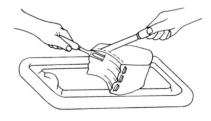

To remove the meat slice, slide the knife blade under the cut slice of meat. Holding it steady with the long-handled meat fork, lift the slice and place it on a platter.

Steak Diane

2 large well-trimmed
  boneless beef top loin
  steaks, 1 inch thick,
  cut in half crosswise
  (about 1¼ pounds
  total) *or* 1 boneless
  beef top sirloin steak,
  cut into 4 serving
  pieces
½ teaspoon freshly
  ground black pepper,
  divided
3 tablespoons butter,
  divided
2 tablespoons Dijon-style
  mustard
2 tablespoons
  Worcestershire sauce
8 ounces fresh oyster or
  crimini mushrooms,
  wiped clean
½ cup chopped shallots or
  sweet onion (page 18)
2 tablespoons brandy or
  cognac
⅔ cup heavy cream
1½ teaspoons chopped
  fresh thyme *or*
  ½ teaspoon dried
  thyme leaves, crushed
  Baked potatoes
  (optional)
  Basil flowers and
  geranium leaves for
  garnish

1. Sprinkle steaks with ¼ teaspoon pepper. Melt 1 tablespoon butter in large skillet over medium-high heat. Add steaks. Cook 2 minutes per side or until browned. Reduce heat to medium; cook 3 to 4 minutes more per side for medium-rare or to desired doneness.

2. Transfer steaks to large shallow dish; spread mustard over both sides of steaks. Spoon Worcestershire sauce over steaks.

3. Slice oyster mushrooms in half with chef's knife; slice crimini mushrooms.

4. Melt remaining 2 tablespoons butter in same skillet over medium heat. Add shallots; cook and stir 4 minutes. Add mushrooms; cook 5 minutes or until mushrooms are softened. Add brandy to skillet; carefully ignite brandy with lighted long match or barbecue starter flame. Let flames burn off alcohol

30 seconds or until flames subside.

5. Stir in cream, thyme and remaining ¼ teaspoon pepper. Cook about 3 minutes or until sauce thickens. Return steaks and Worcestershire mixture to skillet. Cook 3 minutes or until heated through, turning once. Serve steaks with baked potatoes. Spoon sauce over steaks. Garnish, if desired.

Makes 4 servings

Szechuan Grilled Flank Steak

1 piece fresh ginger
(about 1-inch square)
1 beef flank steak (1¼ to
1½ pounds)
¼ cup soy sauce
¼ cup seasoned rice
vinegar
2 tablespoons Asian
sesame oil
4 cloves garlic, minced
(page 52)
½ teaspoon crushed red
pepper flakes
2 to 3 teaspoons sesame
seeds
¼ cup water
½ cup thinly sliced green
onions
Hot cooked rice
(optional)

1. To mince ginger, peel with vegetable peeler and chop with paring knife until ginger is in uniform fine pieces. Mince enough ginger to measure 2 teaspoons.

2. Place steak in large resealable plastic food storage bag. Combine soy sauce, vinegar, oil, garlic, 2 teaspoons ginger and red pepper in cup; pour over steak. Seal bag; turn to coat.

Marinate in refrigerator 3 hours, turning once.

3. Prepare barbecue grill for direct cooking (technique on page 43).

4. Drain steak, reserving marinade in small saucepan. Place steak on grid. Grill, on covered grill, over medium-hot coals 14 to 18 minutes for medium or to desired doneness, turning steak halfway through grilling time.

5. Meanwhile to toast sesame seeds, spread seeds in large, dry skillet. Shake skillet over medium-low heat about 3 minutes or until seeds begin to pop and turn golden. Remove to small bowl; set aside.

6. Add water to reserved marinade. Bring to a boil over high heat. Reduce heat to low; simmer 5 minutes.

7. Transfer steak to carving board. Thinly slice steak across grain into thin slices with large chef's knife, holding knife at 45° angle to cutting board (technique on page 11).

8. Drizzle steak with boiled marinade. Sprinkle with green onions and reserved sesame seeds. Serve with rice.

Makes 4 to 6 servings

Smoky Barbecued Beef Sandwiches

2 large onions
1 well-trimmed first cut
    whole beef brisket
    (about 3 pounds)
½ teaspoon salt
¾ cup beer (not dark)
½ cup firmly packed light
    brown sugar
½ cup ketchup
1 tablespoon plus
    1½ teaspoons
    Worcestershire sauce
1 tablespoon plus
    1½ teaspoons soy
    sauce
2 cloves garlic, minced
    (page 52)
2 whole canned chipotle
    peppers in adobo
    sauce, finely
    chopped*
1 teaspoon adobo sauce
    from can**
6 hoagie or kaiser rolls,
    split and toasted

*Canned chipotle peppers can
be found in the Mexican
section of most supermarkets
or gourmet food stores.

**For spicier flavor, add 1 to
2 teaspoons additional sauce.

1. Preheat oven to 325°F.
To slice onions, slice off
stem and root ends; discard.
Peel away skins. Cut onions
into thin slices with chef's
knife; separate into rings.
Place in bottom of large
roasting pan.

2. Place brisket, fat side up,
over onions; sprinkle with
salt. Combine remaining
ingredients except rolls in
2- or 4-cup glass measuring
cup; pour over brisket.

3. Cover with heavy-duty
foil or roasting pan lid.
Roast in oven 3 to 3½ hours
until brisket is fork-tender.

4. Transfer brisket to cutting
board, leaving sauce in
pan; tent brisket with foil. Let
stand 10 minutes. (Brisket and
sauce may be prepared to this
point; cool and cover
separately. Refrigerate up to
1 day before serving.)

5. Skim fat from pan
juices with large spoon
(technique on page 56);
discard. Transfer juices to
large saucepan. Cook over
medium heat until thickened,
stirring frequently.

6. Trim fat from brisket;
carve across grain into
thin slices with carving knife
(technique on page 11).

7. Return slices to sauce;
cook until heated
through, coating slices with
sauce. Serve slices and sauce
in rolls.

Makes 6 servings

Mustard Crusted Rib Roast

1 (3-rib) standing beef rib roast, trimmed* (6 to 7 pounds)

3 tablespoons Dijon-style mustard

1½ tablespoons chopped fresh tarragon *or* 1½ teaspoons dried tarragon leaves

3 cloves garlic, minced (page 52)

2 shallots

¼ cup dry red wine

1 tablespoon all-purpose flour

1 cup canned single-strength beef broth

Mashed potatoes (optional)

Fresh tarragon sprigs for garnish

*Ask meat retailer to remove chine bone for easier carving. Trim fat to ¼-inch thickness.

1. Preheat oven to 450°F. Place roast, bone side down (the bones take the place of a meat rack), in shallow roasting pan. Combine mustard, chopped tarragon and garlic in small bowl; spread over all surfaces of roast, but not on bottom. Insert meat thermometer into thickest part of roast, not touching bone or fat (technique on page 20). Roast in oven 10 minutes.

2. *Reduce oven temperature to 325°F.* Roast about 20 minutes per pound or until thermometer registers 120° to 130°F for rare or 135° to 145°F for medium.

3. Transfer roast to cutting board; tent with foil. Let stand in warm place 15 minutes for easier carving. (Temperature of roast will rise about 10° during stand time.)

4. Meanwhile, remove papery outer skin from shallots. Cut off root ends. Finely chop enough shallot with utility knife to measure ⅓ cup (technique on page 26).

5. To make gravy, pour fat from roasting pan, reserving 1 tablespoon in medium saucepan. Add wine to roasting pan; place over 2 burners. Cook over medium heat 2 minutes or until slightly thickened, stirring to scrape up browned bits.

6. Add shallots to drippings in saucepan; cook and stir over medium heat 4 minutes or until softened. Add flour; cook and stir 1 minute. Add broth and reserved wine mixture; cook 5 minutes or until sauce thickens, stirring occasionally. Pour through strainer into gravy boat, pressing with back of spoon on shallots; discard.

7. Carve roast into ½-inch-thick slices (technique on page 11). Serve with mashed potatoes and gravy. Garnish, if desired.

Makes 6 to 8 servings

Roasted Herb & Garlic Tenderloin

1 well-trimmed beef
   tenderloin roast (3 to
   4 pounds)
1 tablespoon black
   peppercorns
2 tablespoons chopped
   fresh basil *or*
   2 teaspoons dried
   basil leaves, crushed
1½ tablespoons chopped
   fresh thyme *or*
   1½ teaspoons dried
   thyme leaves, crushed
1 tablespoon chopped
   fresh rosemary *or*
   1 teaspoon dried
   rosemary, crushed
1 tablespoon minced
   garlic (page 52)
   Salt and black pepper
   (optional)

1. Preheat oven to 425°F.

2. To hold shape of roast, tie roast with cotton string in 1½-inch intervals.

3. Place peppercorns in small heavy resealable plastic food storage bag. Squeeze out excess air; seal bag tightly. Pound peppercorns with flat side of meat mallet or rolling pin until cracked.

4. Place roast on meat rack in shallow roasting pan. Combine cracked peppercorns, basil, thyme, rosemary and garlic in small bowl; rub over top surface of roast.

5. Insert meat thermometer into thickest part of roast.

6. Roast in oven 40 to 50 minutes until thermometer registers 125° to 130°F for rare or 135° to 145°F for medium-rare, depending on thickness of roast.

7. Transfer roast to carving board; tent with foil. Let stand 10 minutes before carving. Remove string; discard.

8. To serve, carve crosswise into ½-inch-thick slices with large carving knife (technique on page 11). Season with salt and pepper.

Makes 10 to 12 servings

Beef Stroganoff

8 ounces uncooked egg
    noodles
¼ cup all-purpose flour
½ teaspoon salt
¼ teaspoon black pepper
1¼ pounds beef tenderloin
    tips or tenderloin,
    ½ inch thick
¼ cup butter, divided
¾ cup chopped onion
    (page 26)
12 ounces fresh button
    mushrooms, cleaned,
    wiped and sliced
1 can (10½ ounces)
    condensed beef broth
2 tablespoons tomato
    paste
1 tablespoon
    Worcestershire sauce
1 cup sour cream, at
    room temperature
    Fresh chives for garnish

1. Cook noodles according to package directions; drain and keep warm.

2. Meanwhile, combine flour, salt and pepper in large resealable plastic food storage bag. Cut beef into 1½×½-inch strips with chef's knife; add ½ of beef to flour mixture. Seal bag; shake to coat well (technique on page 24). Repeat with remaining beef.

3. Melt 1 tablespoon butter in large nonstick skillet over medium-high heat. Add ½ of beef mixture to skillet. Cook and stir until browned on all sides. (Do not overcook.) Transfer to medium bowl. Repeat with 1 tablespoon butter and remaining beef mixture; transfer to same bowl. Set aside.

4. Melt remaining 2 tablespoons butter in same skillet over medium-high heat. Add onion; cook 5 minutes, stirring occasionally. Add mushrooms; cook and stir 5 minutes or until mushrooms are tender and release their liquid.

5. Stir in broth, tomato paste and Worcestershire sauce; bring to a boil, scraping up any browned bits.

6. Return beef mixture and any accumulated juices to skillet; cook about 5 minutes or until heated through and sauce thickens. Stir in sour cream; heat through. (Do not boil.)

7. Serve beef mixture over reserved noodles. Garnish, if desired.

Makes 4 servings

Hungarian Beef Goulash

¼ cup all-purpose flour
1 tablespoon Hungarian
sweet paprika
1½ teaspoons salt
½ teaspoon Hungarian hot
paprika
½ teaspoon black pepper
2 pounds beef stew meat
(1¼-inch pieces)
4 tablespoons vegetable
oil, divided
1 large onion, chopped
(page 26)
3 cloves garlic, minced
(page 52)
2 cans (about 14 ounces
each) single-strength
beef broth
1 can (14½ ounces)
stewed tomatoes,
undrained
1 cup water
1 tablespoon dried
marjoram leaves,
crushed
1 large green bell pepper
3 cups uncooked thin egg
noodle twists
Sour cream

1. Combine flour, sweet paprika, salt, hot paprika and black pepper in resealable plastic food storage bag. Add ½ of beef. Seal bag; shake to coat well. Repeat with remaining beef.

2. Heat 1½ tablespoons oil in Dutch oven over medium heat until hot. Add ½ of beef; brown on all sides. Transfer to large bowl. Repeat with 1½ tablespoons oil and remaining beef; transfer to same bowl.

3. Heat remaining 1 tablespoon oil in same Dutch oven; add onion and garlic. Cook 8 minutes or until tender, stirring often.

4. Return beef and any juices to Dutch oven. Add broth, tomatoes with liquid, water and marjoram. Bring to a boil over medium-high heat. Reduce heat to medium-low; cover and simmer 1½ hours or until meat is tender, stirring once.

5. To prepare bell pepper, make circular cut around top of pepper with paring knife. Pull stem from pepper to remove stem, seeds and membrane; discard.

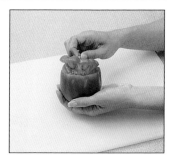

6. Rinse pepper under running water to remove any excess seeds. Slice pepper lengthwise in half on cutting board. Thinly slice each half into strips with chef's knife; chop strips.

7. When meat is tender, stir in bell pepper and noodles; cover. Simmer about 8 minutes or until noodles are tender, stirring once. To serve, ladle into 8 soup bowls. Dollop with sour cream.

Makes 8 servings

Cajun-Style Beef Soup

1 large onion
2 tablespoons vegetable oil
½ cup thinly sliced celery
3 cloves garlic, minced (page 52)
3 pounds beef shank cross cuts, cut 1 inch thick
4 cups water
1 can (10½ ounces) condensed beef broth
1 tablespoon paprika, preferably Hungarian
2 teaspoons salt
1 teaspoon dried thyme leaves, crushed
½ teaspoon ground white pepper
½ teaspoon ground red pepper
¼ teaspoon freshly ground black pepper
1 bay leaf
1 cup thinly sliced peeled carrots
½ cup finely chopped green bell pepper (page 24)
½ cup finely chopped red bell pepper
½ cup long grain white rice, preferably converted
Hot pepper sauce (optional)
Celery leaves and fresh thyme sprigs for garnish

1. To chop onion, peel skin. Cut onion in half through root end with utility knife. Place, cut side down, on cutting board. Cut onion into slices perpendicular to root end, holding onion with fingers to keep its shape; turn and cut crosswise. (The closer the cuts are spaced, the finer the onion will be chopped.) Repeat with remaining onion half.

2. Heat oil in Dutch oven over medium heat until hot; add onion, celery and garlic. Cook 8 minutes, stirring occasionally.

3. Add shanks, water, broth, paprika, salt, dried thyme, ground peppers and bay leaf. Bring to a boil over medium-high heat. Reduce heat to medium-low; cover and simmer 1 hour, stirring occasionally.

4. Remove shanks from soup to cutting board. Remove meat from bones with utility knife. Cut meat into ½-inch pieces.

5. Skim fat from soup with spoon (technique on page 56). Return meat to soup.

6. Add carrots, bell peppers and rice to soup. Bring to a boil over medium-high heat. Reduce heat to medium-low; cover and simmer 45 minutes or until meat is tender. Remove bay leaf; discard.

7. Ladle into 6 individual serving bowls. Serve with hot pepper sauce. Garnish, if desired.

Makes 6 servings

Note: Soup may be covered and refrigerated up to 5 days or stored in an airtight container and frozen up to 3 months.

Beef Mole Tamale Pie

1½ **pounds ground chuck**
1 **medium onion, chopped**
1 **green bell pepper,**
   chopped (page 24)
2 **cloves garlic, minced**
1¼ **cups medium-hot salsa**
1 **package (10 ounces)**
   frozen whole kernel
   corn, partially thawed
1 **tablespoon**
   unsweetened cocoa
   powder
2 **teaspoons ground**
   cumin
1 **teaspoon dried oregano**
   leaves
1½ **teaspoons salt, divided**
¼ **teaspoon ground**
   cinnamon
2 **cups (8 ounces)**
   shredded Monterey
   Jack or Cheddar
   cheese
⅓ **cup chopped fresh**
   cilantro
1 **cup all-purpose flour**
¾ **cup yellow cornmeal**
3 **tablespoons sugar**
2 **teaspoons baking**
   powder
⅔ **cup milk**
3 **tablespoons butter,**
   melted
1 **egg, beaten**
   Chopped tomato, diced
   avocado, chili peppers
   and sour cream for
   garnish

1. Preheat oven to 400°F. Spray 11×7-inch baking dish with nonstick cooking spray.

2. Brown ground chuck with onion, bell pepper and garlic in large deep skillet or Dutch oven over medium heat until meat just loses its pink color, stirring often with wooden spoon to break meat into ½-inch pieces. Pour off drippings.

3. Stir in salsa, corn, cocoa, cumin, oregano, 1 teaspoon salt and cinnamon. Bring to a boil. Reduce heat to medium-low; simmer, uncovered, 8 minutes, stirring occasionally. Remove from heat; stir in cheese and cilantro. Spread in prepared dish.

4. Combine flour, cornmeal, sugar, baking powder and remaining ½ teaspoon salt in large bowl. Add milk, butter and egg; stir just until dry ingredients are moistened.

5. Drop by spoonfuls evenly over meat mixture; spread batter evenly with spatula.

6. Bake 15 minutes. *Reduce oven temperature to 350°F.* Bake 20 minutes or until topping is light brown and filling is bubbly. Let stand 5 minutes before serving. Garnish, if desired.

Makes 6 servings

Italian Meatballs

1½ **pounds meat loaf mix***
   or lean ground beef
⅓ **cup dry bread crumbs**
⅓ **cup milk**
⅓ **cup grated onion**
¼ **cup (1 ounce) freshly**
   grated Parmesan
   cheese
1 **egg**
2 **cloves garlic, minced**
   (page 52)
1½ **teaspoons dried basil**
   leaves
1 **teaspoon salt**
1 **teaspoon dried oregano**
   leaves
½ **teaspoon rubbed sage**
¼ **teaspoon crushed red**
   pepper flakes
   Marinara Sauce (recipe
   follows)
   Additional grated
   Parmesan cheese and
   hot cooked pasta
   (optional)
   Fresh basil sprigs for
   garnish

*Meat loaf mix is a combination of ground beef, pork and veal; see your meat retailer or make your own with 1 pound lean ground beef, ¼ pound pork and ¼ pound veal.

1. Preheat oven to 400°F. Spray broiler pan with nonstick cooking spray.

2. Combine all ingredients except Marinara Sauce, additional cheese and basil sprigs in large bowl. Mix lightly but thoroughly. Shape to form meatballs using ⅓ cup meat mixture for each meatball.

3. Place meatballs on prepared pan; bake 25 to 30 minutes until instant-read thermometer inserted into meatballs registers 145°F.

4. Meanwhile, prepare Marinara Sauce.

5. Add cooked meatballs to Marinara Sauce; simmer, uncovered, about 10 minutes or until meatballs are cooked through and no longer pink in centers, turning meatballs in sauce once. (Internal temperature should register 160° to 165°F.)

6. Serve meatballs in shallow bowls; top with sauce. Serve with cheese and pasta. Garnish, if desired.

Makes 5 to 6 servings

Marinara Sauce

1½ **tablespoons olive oil**
3 **cloves garlic, minced**
1 **can (28 ounces) Italian**
   plum tomatoes,
   undrained
¼ **cup tomato paste**
2 **teaspoons dried basil**
   leaves
½ **teaspoon sugar**
¼ **teaspoon salt**
¼ **teaspoon crushed red**
   pepper flakes

Heat oil in large skillet over medium heat. Add garlic; cook and stir 3 minutes. Stir in remaining ingredients. Bring to a boil. Reduce heat to low; simmer, uncovered, 10 minutes.

Makes about 3½ cups

Tip: If serving with pasta, double sauce recipe.

Veal Chops with Brandied Apricots and Pecans

8 **dried apricot halves**
¼ **cup water**
¼ **cup honey**
4 **(¾-inch-thick) boneless veal chops (about 5 ounces each)***
¼ **teaspoon salt**
¼ **teaspoon freshly ground black pepper**
3 **tablespoons all-purpose flour**
2 **tablespoons butter or margarine**
16 **pecan halves**
2 **tablespoons brandy Celery or mint leaves for garnish**

*If boneless chops are unavailable, chops with bones may be substituted.

1. Cut apricot halves into ¼-inch slivers with utility knife.

2. Combine water and honey in 2-cup glass measuring cup; microwave on HIGH (100% power) 2 minutes or until mixture begins to boil. Stir in slivered apricots; cover with plastic wrap, turning back 1 corner to vent. Microwave 30 seconds more; let stand, covered, 1 hour.

3. Meanwhile, sprinkle veal chops with salt and pepper. Place flour in shallow bowl; dredge veal chops, 1 at a time, in flour, shaking off excess.

4. Melt butter in large skillet over medium heat; arrange veal chops and pecan halves in single layer in skillet. Cook veal chops and pecans 5 minutes per side or until browned.

5. Add apricot mixture and brandy; bring to a boil. Reduce heat to low; cover and simmer 10 minutes or until veal chops are tender.

6. Transfer veal chops and pecans to 4 warm serving plates with slotted spatula. Bring apricot mixture in skillet to a boil over high heat; cook 1 minute or until slightly thickened. To serve, spoon apricot mixture over veal chops. Garnish, if desired.

Makes 4 servings

Veal Cordon Bleu

Strawberry Insalata
(recipe follows)
4 thin veal cutlets or veal
scaloppine (4 ounces
each)
Salt and black pepper
1 egg, beaten
1 tablespoon milk
4 slices prosciutto or
cooked ham (½ ounce
each)
2 slices Swiss or Gruyère
cheese (1 ounce
each), cut in half
1 cup seasoned fine dry
bread crumbs
½ cup all-purpose flour
2 tablespoons olive oil
Lemon balm for garnish

1. Prepare Strawberry
Insalata; refrigerate.

2. Place each veal cutlet
between sheets of
waxed paper on cutting board.
Pound each cutlet with meat
mallet to ⅛- to ¼-inch
thickness. (Omit step if using
scaloppine.)

3. Lightly sprinkle 1 side of
each cutlet with salt and
pepper. Whisk together egg
and milk in small bowl.

4. Place 1 prosciutto slice
and 1 cheese slice half
in center of each veal piece.
Brush tops of cheese and
edges of veal with milk mixture.

5. Fold long edges of veal
over prosciutto and
cheese, pressing gently to
adhere. Beginning at short
ends, roll veal jelly-roll
fashion. Secure with wooden
picks.

6. Place bread crumbs and
flour on separate plates.
Roll veal in flour, then dip in
milk mixture. Roll veal in
bread crumbs, pressing to
coat well. Place on ungreased
baking sheet; cover and
refrigerate 1 hour.

7. Heat oil in large skillet
over medium-high heat
until hot. Add veal; cook
20 minutes, turning veal
¼ turn every 5 minutes, or
until veal is tender and barely
pink in center. Remove
toothpicks; discard. Serve
immediately with Strawberry
Insalata. Garnish, if desired.

Makes 4 servings

Strawberry Insalata

3 cups hulled, sliced fresh
strawberries
3 tablespoons sugar
2 tablespoons balsamic
vinegar
Dash salt and ground
red pepper

Combine all ingredients in
medium glass bowl, stirring
well. Place in 4 individual
serving dishes. Cover with
plastic wrap; refrigerate at
least 1 hour and no more than
2 hours.

Makes 2 cups

Veal Piccata with Fennel

8 thin veal cutlets or veal scaloppine (about 2 ounces each)
½ teaspoon fennel seeds
Salt and freshly ground black pepper
½ cup all-purpose flour
2 tablespoons olive oil, divided
2 tablespoons butter, divided
2 lemons
2 tablespoons white wine
2 tablespoons chopped fresh parsley
Lemon wedges for garnish

1. Pound veal with meat mallet on cutting board to ⅛-inch thickness (technique on page 34).

2. Crush fennel seeds in mortar with pestle. Or, place seeds in small resealable plastic food storage bag. Squeeze out excess air; seal bag tightly. Crush with wooden mallet.

3. Sprinkle 1 side of each veal cutlet with crushed fennel seeds; season to taste with salt and pepper. Place flour in shallow bowl. Lightly coat veal pieces with flour. (Discard leftover flour.)

4. Heat 1 tablespoon each oil and butter in large skillet over medium-high heat until butter is bubbly. Add ½ of floured veal; cook about 1 minute per side or until veal is tender. Drain well on paper towels. Repeat procedure with remaining oil, butter and floured veal. (Do not drain skillet.)

5. Cut lemons crosswise in half; squeeze with citrus reamer to extract juice into cup. Combine juice and wine in small bowl.

6. To deglaze skillet, pour juice mixture into skillet. Cook over medium-high heat, scraping up any browned bits and stirring frequently.

7. Return veal to skillet; sprinkle with parsley and heat through. Transfer veal and sauce to warm serving plates. Garnish, if desired.

Makes 4 servings

Roasted Pork Tenderloin with Fresh Plum Salsa

2 to 3 limes
Fresh Plum Salsa
(recipe follows)
1 whole well-trimmed
pork tenderloin (about
1 pound)
⅓ cup soy sauce
1 tablespoon Asian
sesame oil
2 cloves garlic, minced
(page 52)
2 tablespoons firmly
packed brown sugar
Fresh cilantro sprigs
and lime wedges for
garnish

1. Cut limes crosswise in half; squeeze with citrus reamer to extract juice into measuring cup. Measure 2 tablespoons; set aside. Prepare Fresh Plum Salsa using remaining juice.

2. Place tenderloin in large resealable plastic food storage bag. Combine soy sauce, 2 tablespoons lime juice, oil and garlic in small bowl. Pour over tenderloin. Seal bag tightly, turning to coat (technique on page 54).

Marinate in refrigerator overnight, turning occasionally.

3. Preheat oven to 375°F. Drain tenderloin, reserving 2 tablespoons marinade. Combine reserved marinade and sugar in small saucepan. Bring to a boil over medium-high heat. Cook 1 minute, stirring once; set aside.

4. To ensure even cooking, tuck narrow end of tenderloin under roast, forming even thickness of meat. Secure with cotton string. Place tenderloin on meat rack in shallow roasting pan. Brush with reserved sugar mixture.

5. Insert meat thermometer into tenderloin. Bake 15 minutes; brush with remaining sugar mixture. Bake 10 minutes more or until thermometer registers 160°F.

6. Transfer tenderloin to cutting board; tent with foil (technique on page 20). Let stand 10 minutes. Remove string from tenderloin; discard. Carve tenderloin into thin slices with carving knife (technique on page 11). Serve with Fresh Plum Salsa. Garnish, if desired.

Makes 4 servings

Fresh Plum Salsa

2 cups coarsely chopped
red plums (about 3)
2 tablespoons chopped
green onion
2 tablespoons firmly
packed brown sugar
1 tablespoon chopped
fresh cilantro
2 teaspoons freshly
squeezed lime juice
Dash ground red pepper

Combine all ingredients in small bowl. Cover; refrigerate at least 2 hours.

Makes 1 cup

Pilaf-Stuffed Pork Loin Roast

5 tablespoons butter or
  margarine, divided
¼ cup chopped onion
  (page 26)
¼ cup chopped celery
1 clove garlic, minced
  (page 52)
2 cups chicken broth
1 cup uncooked long
  grain and wild rice
  blend
½ cup finely chopped
  pecans
3 tablespoons orange
  marmalade
4 teaspoons dried whole
  leaf thyme, divided
¾ teaspoon salt
½ teaspoon freshly
  ground black pepper
1 boneless, rolled and
  tied pork loin roast
  (5 to 6 pounds)*
1 onion, sliced and
  separated into rings
  (page 16)
½ cup water
1 tablespoon vegetable
  oil
2 tablespoons soy sauce
  Orange juice
2 tablespoons all-purpose
  flour
  Plum slices and fresh
  chervil for garnish

*Ask your meat retailer to try
and keep the roast in 1 piece
when boning.

1. Preheat oven to 350°F.
Melt 2 tablespoons butter
in medium saucepan over
medium heat; stir in chopped
onion, celery and garlic. Cook
until onion is tender, stirring
frequently. Add broth; bring to
a boil. Stir in rice blend.

Reduce heat to low; cover and
simmer 20 minutes. Remove
from heat; let stand
5 minutes or until all liquid is
absorbed.

2. Meanwhile to toast
pecans, spread in single
layer on baking sheet. Bake
6 to 8 minutes until lightly
browned, stirring often.

3. *Reduce oven
temperature to 325°F.*
Add pecans, marmalade,
1 teaspoon thyme, salt and
pepper to rice blend; toss
gently until blended. Cover;
set aside.

4. Cut and remove strings
from roast; discard. To
butterfly roast, split roast in
half where the 2 pieces fall
apart. (If possible, keep roast
in 1 piece.)

5. To butterfly each roast
half, make horizontal cut
starting from center crease of
roast to within 1 inch of
opposite edge. (If roast is in
2 pieces, butterfly 1 piece
through center.) Open roast
half and press uncut edge to
flatten as much as possible.

6. Butterfly remaining roast
half, starting from center
crease and cutting to but not
through outside edge.

continued on page 42

Pilaf-Stuffed Pork Loin Roast, *continued*

Open both sides of roast to obtain 1 piece with four sections of uniform thickness. (If roast is in 2 pieces, secure with wooden picks.)

7. Spoon rice mixture over roast, leaving 1-inch border. Cut enough heavy cotton string to tie roast at 1-inch intervals, making sure strings are long enough to tie securely. Place strings under roast. Beginning with 1 long side, roll roast jelly-roll fashion and tie with strings, being careful to keep 2 pieces together if necessary. Tie entire roast lengthwise with additional string.

8. Arrange onion rings in single layer in greased shallow roasting pan. Pour water over onion rings. Place meat rack in roasting pan. Place roast on rack; brush with oil and sprinkle with remaining 1 tablespoon thyme. Insert meat thermometer into thickest part of roast but not in rice stuffing (technique on page 20).

9. Cover with foil; roast in oven 2½ hours or until meat thermometer registers 160°F (about 30 minutes per pound). Remove foil during last 30 minutes of roasting.

10. Carefully transfer roast to serving platter; tent with foil. Remove onion rings from roasting pan; discard. Let roast stand 10 minutes. Meanwhile, to deglaze pan, pour soy sauce into pan drippings. Cook over medium-high heat, scraping up any browned bits and stirring frequently (technique on page 36). Transfer mixture to deglazing measuring cup; let stand until fat rises to surface. Pour mixture into 2- or 4-cup measuring cup, stopping short of risen fat. (If deglazing

measuring cup is unavailable, spoon fat from surface.) Add orange juice to measuring cup to equal 1¼ cups; set aside.

11. Melt remaining 3 tablespoons butter in small saucepan over medium heat; add flour, stirring until blended with wire whisk. Add orange juice mixture; cook until thickened and bubbly, stirring frequently. Season with additional salt and black pepper, if desired.

12. Remove strings from roast; discard. Carve roast (technique on page 11) and serve with orange juice mixture. Garnish, if desired.

Makes 12 servings

Fiery Grilled Buffalo-Style Chops and Vegetables

**Zesty Blue Cheese
  Butter (page 44)
4 medium baking
  potatoes
Vegetable oil
2 medium-size red bell
  peppers
4 (¾-inch-thick) boneless
  pork loin chops
  (about 4 ounces each)
⅓ cup butter or margarine
⅓ cup hot pepper sauce
Prepared coleslaw
  (optional)**

1. Prepare Zesty Blue Cheese Butter up to 2 days in advance; refrigerate.

2. Preheat oven to 375°F. Scrub potatoes under cold running water with soft vegetable brush; rinse well. Pierce each potato in several places with fork. Pat potatoes dry with paper towels; rub skins with oil. Bake 1 hour or until just fork-tender. While hot, cut potatoes lengthwise in half. Cool to room temperature.

3. Meanwhile to seed bell pepper, cut pepper lengthwise in half with chef's knife. Scrape out and discard stem, seeds and membrane with spoon, being careful not to cut through shell. Rinse under cold running water. Repeat with remaining bell pepper; set aside.

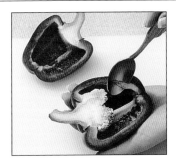

4. To prepare grill for direct cooking, arrange coals in pyramid shape about 20 to 30 minutes prior to grilling or preheat broiler. (There should be enough charcoal so that when it is spread in single layer, it will extend 1 to 2 inches beyond area of food on grid.) Soak coals with about ½ cup lighter fluid. Wait 1 minute for coals to soak; light with match. (Electric starter or chimney starter also may be used. Follow manufacturer's directions.)

5. Trim excess fat from pork chops with utility knife, if necessary. Place pork chops, bell pepper halves and potatoes in jumbo-size resealable plastic food storage bag. Melt butter in small saucepan over low heat. Stir in pepper sauce; pour over chops, bell peppers and potatoes. Seal bag tightly; turn to coat. Marinate at room temperature no more than 15 minutes, turning once (technique on page 54).

6. Coals are ready when they are about 80% ash gray during daylight and glow at night. When coals are ready, spread in single layer with barbecue tongs.

continued on page 44

Fiery Grilled Buffalo-Style Chops and Vegetables, continued

7. Carefully place chops and vegetables on grid with clean tongs, reserving marinade in small saucepan. Grill, on uncovered grill, over medium-high coals or broil, 4 inches from heat, on foil-lined jelly-roll pan 5 minutes. Turn chops and vegetables and baste once with reserved marinade; discard any remaining marinade. Cook 5 minutes more or until pork is barely pink in center. (Do not overcook or pork will be dry. Instant-read thermometer inserted into center of pork should register 160°F.)

8. Transfer chops and vegetables to 4 individual serving plates. Serve with slices of Zesty Blue Cheese Butter and coleslaw.

Makes 4 servings

Zesty Blue Cheese Butter

4 ounces blue cheese, such as Gorgonzola or Roquefort
½ cup butter or margarine, softened
1 package (3 ounces) cream cheese, softened
2 tablespoons finely chopped green onion
2 slices bacon, cooked, drained and crumbled

1. Crumble blue cheese with fingers to measure 1 cup; place in small bowl.

2. Add butter and cream cheese; beat with electric mixer at medium speed until smooth, scraping side of bowl as necessary. Stir in onion and bacon.

3. Place butter mixture on sheet of waxed paper. Using waxed paper, roll mixture back and forth into 8-inch log.

4. Wrap waxed paper around butter log to seal. Refrigerate at least 1 hour or up to 2 days.

Makes about 1 cup

Jamaican Baby Back Ribs

2 tablespoons sugar
2 tablespoons fresh
  lemon juice (page 36)
1 tablespoon salt
1 tablespoon vegetable
  oil
2 teaspoons black pepper
2 teaspoons dried thyme
  leaves, crushed
¾ teaspoon *each* ground
  cinnamon, nutmeg
  and allspice
½ teaspoon ground red
  pepper
6 pounds well-trimmed
  pork baby back ribs,
  cut into 3- to 4-rib
  portions
  Barbecue Sauce (recipe
  follows)

1. For seasoning rub, combine all ingredients except ribs and Barbecue Sauce in small bowl; stir well. Spread over all surfaces of ribs; press with fingertips so mixture adheres to ribs. Cover; refrigerate overnight.

2. To prepare grill for indirect cooking, place rectangular metal or disposable foil drip pan in grill; bank coals either to one side or both sides of pan.

3. Soak coals with about ½ cup lighter fluid. Wait 1 minute for coals to soak; light with match.

4. While coals are heating, prepare Barbecue Sauce.

5. Coals are ready when they are about 80% ash gray during daylight and glow at night. Place seasoned ribs directly on cooking grid over drip pan. Grill, covered, 1 hour, turning occasionally.

6. Baste ribs generously with Barbecue Sauce; grill 30 minutes more or until ribs are tender and browned, turning occasionally.

7. Bring remaining Barbecue Sauce to a boil over medium-high heat; boil 1 minute. Serve ribs with remaining sauce.

Makes 6 servings

Barbecue Sauce

  2 tablespoons butter
½ cup finely chopped
    onion (page 26)
1½ cups ketchup
  1 cup red currant jelly
¼ cup apple cider vinegar
  1 tablespoon soy sauce
¼ teaspoon *each* ground
    red and black peppers

Melt butter in medium saucepan over medium-high heat. Add onion; cook and stir until softened. Stir in remaining ingredients. Reduce heat to medium-low; simmer 20 minutes, stirring often.

Makes about 3 cups

Ovenbaked Jamaican Ribs: Preheat oven to 350°F. Prepare ribs as directed in step 1. Place ribs in foil-lined roasting pan. Cover with foil; bake 1 hour. Uncover; baste with Barbecue Sauce. Bake, uncovered, 30 minutes more. Continue as directed in step 7.

Baked Holiday Ham with Cranberry-Wine Compote

2 teaspoons peanut oil
⅔ cup chopped onion
    (page 26)
½ cup chopped celery
1 cup red wine
1 cup honey
½ cup sugar
1 package (12 ounces)
    fresh cranberries
1 fully-cooked smoked
    ham (10 pounds)
Whole cloves
Kumquats and currant
    leaves for garnish

1. For Cranberry-Wine Compote, heat oil in large saucepan over medium-high heat until hot; add onion and celery. Cook until tender, stirring frequently. Stir in wine, honey and sugar; bring to a boil. Add cranberries; return to a boil. Reduce heat to low; cover and simmer 10 minutes. Cool completely.

2. Carefully ladle enough clear syrup from cranberry mixture into glass measuring cup to equal 1 cup; set aside. Transfer remaining cranberry mixture to serving bowl; cover and refrigerate.

3. Slice away skin from ham with sharp utility knife. (Omit step if meat retailer has already removed skin.)

4. Preheat oven to 325°F. Score fat on ham in diamond design with sharp utility knife; stud with whole cloves.

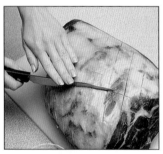

5. Place ham, fat side up, on rack in shallow roasting pan.

6. Bake, uncovered, 1½ hours. Baste ham with reserved cranberry-wine syrup. Insert meat thermometer into thickest part of ham, not touching bone.

Bake 1 to 2 hours more until meat thermometer registers 140°F, basting with cranberry-wine syrup twice.*

7. Let ham stand 10 minutes before transferring to warm serving platter. Slice ham with large carving knife (technique on page 11). Serve warm with chilled Cranberry-Wine Compote. Garnish, if desired.

Makes 16 to 20 servings

*Total cooking time for ham should be 18 to 24 minutes per pound.

Cream-Style Red Beans and Rice

12 ounces dried red beans
½ pound smoked ham
½ pound fully-cooked
  smoked andouille
  sausage or other
  smoked sausage
1½ tablespoons olive oil
1 cup chopped onion
  (page 26)
1 cup chopped green bell
  pepper (page 24)
1 cup chopped celery
2 cloves garlic, minced
  (page 52)
5 cups water
1 teaspoon salt
1 teaspoon dried thyme
  leaves, crushed
½ teaspoon dried oregano
  leaves, crushed
¼ teaspoon black pepper
⅛ teaspoon ground red
  pepper
2 bay leaves
2 tablespoons tomato
  paste
  Hot cooked rice

1. Rinse beans thoroughly in colander under cold running water, picking out debris and any blemished beans. Place beans in large bowl; add water to cover by 2 inches. Cover; let stand at room temperature overnight.

2. Cut ham into ½-inch cubes with utility knife; set aside.

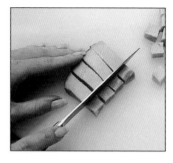

3. Cut sausage into ¼-inch slices with utility knife; set aside.

4. Heat oil in large Dutch oven over medium-high heat until hot. Add onion, bell pepper, celery and garlic; cook and stir 2 minutes. Stir in 5 cups water, reserved ham and seasonings. Bring to a boil. Reduce heat. Cover; simmer 1 hour.

5. Drain beans, discarding soaking water. Add beans to ham mixture; bring to a boil over high heat. Reduce heat to low. Cover; simmer 1 hour or until beans are tender.

6. Carefully ladle 1 cup bean mixture into food processor or blender container. Cover; process until mixture is smooth.

7. Return puréed mixture to Dutch oven; stir in sausage and tomato paste.

8. Cook, uncovered, over medium heat 10 minutes or until thickened and bubbly, stirring occasionally. Remove bay leaves; discard. Serve in bowls over hot cooked rice.

Makes 6 to 8 servings

Herb-Roasted Racks of Lamb

2 to 3 cloves garlic
2 whole racks (6 ribs each) lamb loin chops (2½ to 3 pounds)
½ cup mango chutney, chopped
1 cup fresh French or Italian bread crumbs
1 tablespoon chopped fresh thyme *or* 1 teaspoon dried thyme leaves, crushed
1 tablespoon chopped fresh rosemary *or* 1 teaspoon dried rosemary, crushed
1 tablespoon chopped fresh oregano *or* 1 teaspoon dried oregano

1. Preheat oven to 400°F. To mince garlic, trim ends of cloves; discard. Slightly crush cloves under flat side of chef's knife blade; peel away skin.

2. Chop garlic into uniform fine pieces with chef's knife.

3. Trim fat from racks of lamb with chef's knife on cutting board.

4. Combine chutney and garlic in small bowl; spread evenly over meaty side of lamb with thin spatula. Combine remaining ingredients in separate small bowl; pat crumb mixture evenly over chutney mixture.

5. Place lamb racks, crumb sides up, on rack in shallow roasting pan. Roast in oven about 30 minutes or until instant-read thermometer inserted into lamb, but not touching bone, registers 135°F for rare or to desired doneness.

6. Place lamb on carving board. Slice between ribs into individual chops with large carving knife. Garnish with additional fresh herbs and mango slices, if desired. Serve immediately.

Makes 4 servings

Marinated Grilled Lamb Chops

**8 well-trimmed lamb loin
chops, cut 1 inch
thick (about
2¼ pounds)**
**3 cloves garlic, minced
(page 52)**
**2 tablespoons chopped
fresh rosemary *or*
2 teaspoons dried
rosemary, crushed**
**2 tablespoons chopped
fresh mint leaves *or*
2 teaspoons dried
mint leaves, crushed**
¾ cup dry red wine
**⅓ cup butter or margarine,
softened**
¼ teaspoon salt
**¼ teaspoon freshly
ground black pepper
Fresh mint leaves for
garnish**

1. To marinate, place chops
in large resealable plastic
food storage bag. Combine
garlic, rosemary and chopped
mint in small bowl. Combine
½ of garlic mixture and wine
in glass measuring cup. Pour
wine mixture over chops in
bag. Close bag securely; turn
to coat. Marinate chops in
refrigerator at least 2 hours or
up to 4 hours, turning
occasionally.

2. Add butter, salt and
pepper to remaining
garlic mixture; mix well. Spoon
onto center of sheet of plastic
wrap. Using plastic wrap as a
guide, shape butter mixture
into 4×1½-inch log. Wrap
securely in plastic wrap;
refrigerate until ready to
serve.

3. Prepare grill for direct
cooking (technique on
page 43).

4. Drain chops, discarding
marinade. Place chops
on grid. Grill, on covered grill,
over medium coals about
9 minutes or until instant-read
thermometer inserted into
chops registers 160°F for
medium or to desired
doneness, turning once.

5. Cut butter log crosswise
into 8 (½-inch) slices.
To serve, top each chop with
slice of seasoned butter.
Garnish, if desired.

Makes 4 servings

Provençal-Style Lamb Shanks

2 tablespoons olive oil
4 lamb shanks (about
    1 pound each)
2 large onions, chopped
    (page 26)
5 cloves garlic, minced
    (page 52), divided
1 can (28 ounces) Italian-
    style plum tomatoes,
    undrained and
    coarsely chopped
½ cup dry vermouth
1½ teaspoons dried basil
    leaves, crushed
1½ teaspoons dried
    rosemary, crushed
1 teaspoon salt
½ teaspoon freshly
    ground black pepper
1 can (19 ounces)
    cannellini beans,
    rinsed and drained
1½ tablespoons balsamic
    vinegar (optional)
2 tablespoons chopped
    fresh Italian parsley
1 teaspoon grated lemon
    peel
    Fresh lovage leaves and
    lemon peel twists for
    garnish

1. Heat 1 tablespoon oil in Dutch oven over medium heat until hot. Add 2 lamb shanks. Brown on all sides; transfer to large plate with tongs. Repeat with remaining 1 tablespoon oil and 2 lamb shanks.

2. Add onions and 4 cloves garlic to drippings in Dutch oven; cook 6 to 8 minutes until onions are tender, stirring occasionally.

3. Add tomatoes with liquid, vermouth, basil, rosemary, salt and pepper; bring to a boil over medium-high heat. Return shanks to Dutch oven. Reduce heat to low; cover and simmer 1½ hours or until shanks are tender.

4. Remove shanks; cool slightly. Skim fat from pan juices with large spoon; discard.

5. Stir beans into pan juices; heat through. Cut lamb from shanks into 1-inch pieces with utility knife; discard bones and gristle. Return lamb to Dutch oven; heat through. Stir in vinegar.

6. Combine parsley, lemon peel and remaining clove garlic in small bowl. To serve, ladle lamb mixture into 6 individual shallow serving bowls; sprinkle with parsley mixture. Garnish, if desired.

Makes 6 servings (about 10 cups)

Lemon-Garlic Shish Kabobs

1½ **pounds well-trimmed**
   boneless lamb leg
¼ **cup olive oil**
2 **tablespoons fresh**
   lemon juice (page 36)
4 **cloves garlic, minced**
   (page 52)
2 **tablespoons chopped**
   fresh oregano *or*
   2 teaspoons dried
   oregano leaves
½ **teaspoon salt**
½ **teaspoon black pepper**
1 **red or yellow bell**
   pepper, halved and
   seeded (page 43)
1 **small zucchini**
1 **yellow squash**
1 **small red onion**
8 **ounces large fresh**
   button mushrooms,
   wiped clean and
   stems trimmed
   Fresh oregano sprigs
   for garnish

1. Cut lamb into 1¼-inch pieces with large chef's knife.

2. Place lamb in large resealable plastic food storage bag. Combine oil, juice, garlic, chopped oregano, salt and black pepper in glass measuring cup; pour over lamb in bag. Close bag securely; turn to coat. Marinate lamb in refrigerator 1 to 4 hours, turning once (technique on page 54).

3. Prepare grill for direct cooking (technique on page 43).

4. Cut each pepper half into 3 wedges; cut each wedge crosswise in half.

5. Scrub zucchini and yellow squash with vegetable brush under cold running water. Trim tip and stem ends with utility knife; discard. Cut each into 1-inch pieces.

6. Peel onion; cut in half with chef's knife. Place, cut side down, on cutting board; cut each half into ½-inch wedges.

7. Drain lamb, reserving marinade. Alternately thread lamb, bell pepper, zucchini, yellow squash, onion and mushrooms onto 12 (10-inch) metal skewers*; brush both sides with reserved marinade.

8. Place kabobs on grid. Grill, on covered grill, over medium-hot coals 6 minutes. Turn; continue to grill, covered, 5 to 7 minutes for medium or until desired doneness is reached. Garnish, if desired. Serve hot.

Makes 6 servings (2 kabobs each)

*If using bamboo skewers, soak in cold water 10 to 15 minutes to prevent burning.

Greek Lamb Burgers

¼ **cup pine nuts**
 1 **pound lean ground lamb**
¼ **cup finely chopped onion (page 26)**
 3 **cloves garlic, minced (page 52), divided**
¾ **teaspoon salt**
¼ **teaspoon freshly ground black pepper**
¼ **cup plain yogurt**
¼ **teaspoon sugar**
 4 **slices red onion (¼ inch thick)**
 1 **tablespoon olive oil**
 8 **pumpernickel bread slices**
12 **thin cucumber slices**
 4 **tomato slices**

1. Prepare grill for direct cooking (technique on page 43).

2. Meanwhile to toast pine nuts, heat small skillet over medium heat until hot. Add pine nuts; cook 30 to 45 seconds until light brown, shaking pan occasionally.

3. Combine lamb, pine nuts, chopped onion, 2 cloves garlic, salt and pepper in large bowl; mix well. Shape 4 patties, about ½ inch thick and 4 inches in diameter.

4. Combine yogurt, sugar and remaining garlic in small bowl; set aside.

5. Coals are ready when they are about 80% ash gray during daylight and glow at night. When coals are ready, spread in single layer with barbecue tongs.

6. Brush 1 side of each patty and onion slice with oil; place on grid, oil sides down. Brush other sides with oil. Grill, on covered grill, over medium-hot coals 8 to 10 minutes for medium or until desired doneness is reached, turning halfway through grilling time.

7. Place bread on grid to toast during last few minutes of grilling time; grill 1 to 2 minutes per side.

8. Top 4 bread slices with patties and onion slices; top each with 3 cucumber slices and 1 tomato slice. Dollop evenly with yogurt mixture. Close sandwiches with remaining 4 bread slices. Serve immediately.

Makes 4 servings

62

INDEX